Solace

Also by James Cushing

You and the Night and the Music
The Length of an Afternoon
Undercurrent Blues
Pinocchio's Revolution
The Magicians' Union

Solace

Poems by ~~James Cushing~~

James Cushing

for John Schneider —

9/30/21 — Hollywood —

Chris lives!

J

cahuenga
PRESS

This book is dedicated to Celeste Goyer.

Cover photo: Holaday Mason, from "The Urn Series," 2016.
Book design and typesetting: Ellison / Goodreau, Los Angeles, CA
Printed by: McNaughton and Gunn, Inc., Saline, MI, USA.

Gratitude for attentive attention and prompt prompting:
Steve Abee, Lisa Coffman, Brendan Constantine, Iris Cushing, Marsha de la O, Susan Hayden, L. I. Henley, David Kann, Paula Lowe, Phoebe MacAdams, Sarah Maclay, Holaday Mason, Jonathan Maule, Richard Modiano and everyone at Beyond Baroque, Harry Northup, Holly Prado, Chuck Rosenthal, Terrie Silverman, Dian Sousa, Leslie St. John, Gail Wronsky.

First Edition
ISBN: 9780985184339
Library of Congress Control Number: 2018904334

Cahuenga Press is owned, financed and operated by its poet-members James Cushing, Phoebe MacAdams Ozuna, Harry E. Northup and Holly Prado Northup. Our common goal is to create fine books of poetry by poets whose work we admire and respect; to make poetry actual in the world in ways which honor both individual creative freedom and cooperative support.

Cahuenga Press
1256 N. Mariposa Ave.
Los Angeles CA 90029
www.cahuengapress.com

Acknowledgements:

"A Bright Yellow Nap": *Mudfish,* NYC
"A Pillowcase Moon": *The Pedestal,* online
"Everything I Touched": *Third Wednesday,* online
"Memory Kitchenette": *Spectrum* anthology, 2016
"Only in Theory": *Tribeca Review,* NYC
"Reunion": *Permafrost,* Fairbanks AK
(under the title "Sonnet ["the coach...'])
"The Solitary Rider," "One Evening, Years Ago": *LA Cultural Weekly*
"The Unfolding": *Tribeca Poetry Review,* NYC
"Unpublished Cartoon": *Artillery,* LA

John Ashbery died while this collection was in preparation. May the memory of his gentle personal charm and the legacy of his poetry never be forgotten.

Table of Contents

Solace

Unpublished Cartoon

Only streaks could make sections in what waited
to be sectioned, yet nothing waited for streaks.

My mother was a flashlight with wadded tissue paper batteries,
my father was a thin gold timepiece built by

a bleeding lieutenant who learned his craft in a grove
where I have been hiding from you until just now.

Guilty Knowledge

Clown, give me your red rubber nose that I may squeeze it.
This is not a child's dilemma: strange footsteps thump
and we feel more alive than we do in winter.
Little electric lights fall
onto our piñata. I remember
what I wanted to ask my mother

before she rode off on a sticky bronze horse – I never heard
her words, but guessed the size of her happiness,
her power to confuse.
From the back, she's an evergreen
who sees the lilies wilt, sunflowers drop
their seeds and droop,
rocks the size of horses disappear in a single night.
From the front, she's stalking the weekend.
Her coins darken in her palm.

I have one eye for what I'm following, another for the path it takes.
No one but me sees their glowing tracks.

The Unmoored Witness

1.

My mother's fearful of boys at the moment.
Their exaggerated postures bubble
within her (swoon, fight, repeat) as she
tries to finish her fish.
Notice that word
tries. Notice the array of knives around it,
the goose-bump arms.
The port city of her life, where I still awaken,
which still awakens me, retains damage like a tattoo.

I can't think straight while falling past my seated
mother. In her chair, she has replaced herself
with six red roses, each one an entrance
to a kitchen in her past. In these kitchens, I pick
at her casserole, never captioning the
images – a shaman with a lantern, a waterless well,
a bright red 1967 Ford Mustang – that rush
past me as I fall, and keep falling.

2.

In a room with many burning candles, a woman
tosses a red rubber clown nose to a man.

The morning rings with bells they do not hear.
They ring too late, anyway, setting

ripples circling out through the quiet
morning, little wet monsters with a point.

I count the ripples with my feet, not my eyes,
feel hallelujahs igniting in our blood.

In memory, and in our future, where the
heart of our trouble lives, a double bed's the venue

for the blind. But that
takes about a year.

3.

"I slept well but my little mounds of sorrow tore at me like a sharp earring. I stepped into the elevator, rode without a word being spoken to the top floor of a tall building, and walked toward a warm light from a half-opened closet door. No one was around in this dream, but a stand of alder was waving at me from below, to the west. I could see the halo glazing each shrub. The mental effort exhausted me. Yet near that closet, some giant seemed to have fallen over, or a statue of a giant – no, it was still alive, but barely – and I found myself clutching one of its limbs and helping his large family carry his heavy, uncooperative body up to Shell Mound Hill, which was sacred Native turf, and very cold this time of year. Only there, they explained, could the giant's body nourish the earth; 'even sunlight itself,' one elderly woman said, 'must come to feed on the giant's golden tendrils.' Another tribal elder lit a fuse..."

I whisper the word "boom" into your ear, you stir and shake your head. I rest my hand lightly on your moment of awakening, remembering all the mirrors my father kept in the basement of my childhood home...

The Thick Breeze

A ghost convinced my mother I liked ketchup. This happened
years ago, but still. The ghost so convinced everyone
to notice red first, my mother bought me ketchup for
my birthday, for Christmas, even for my Easter basket:
a sweet, tangy red childhood remains her greatest gift to me.

Thank you, ghost, for sharing your ancient names with me.
My last ounce of dignity has leaked all over the national table,
already scattered with pastry crumbs, and
so much has fallen away under this harsh light
I gladden at the sight of the names of extinct birds:
Great Auk, Passenger Pigeon, North Island Laughing Owl.

And now, so many other kinds of life closed off,
we nest in any open field I find,
the ghost and I, coated with everything
we know, and give thanks.

Un Ballo in Maschera

The opera you left here has grown
cold-hearted,
and its shadows fall dark and hard on some shoulders,
some palms.
                    Then the visitor nodded; my initiation dance
was cleared for takeoff, and a servant brought
a woolen blanket. I heard her mutter "three planets
in alignment" as she stepped away from me.
Furniture usurped the role of fingers
but in the center of her palm lay the observer's eye.
The sky lowered, and the winter wind paused to vote yes.

In the future, however, I must behave differently.
These lists of names I'll always love, but milking them the way I do
I see now is wrong.
I know most of what orphans know by now, but
I have learned to look on, quiet,
at all that lies ample before me, knowing something there
keeps counsel with my secrets, down where the sayable
lives with her curtain.
I know she grew legs, then feet and mocking claws,
and then the big men died,
leaving only little ones, whose sons also died.
Now downtown's mother calls out
from on top of her horse, so we can't hear her.
But hearing her isn't our goal right now.

A Bright Yellow Nap

My mother slept with the man who knew
the names of each little cloud of smoke puffing
from underneath her bedroom door, and he
counted her coins at the end of her day. The sky
was so abraded that when I found strands of it in my bed
just after waking I could never tell what it was. The summer'd
been evicted. Moon-illuminated pedestrians gathered
to talk about their sons and sons' hypnotists,

so who is to be thanked for the way we all turned out?
My hands are other people, and my legs and feet
are animals, mating as they walk. A year has passed
since fissures first showed – they're deeper, wider,
bluer. Something adjusts the speed of the shuffle; we're
low on milk, snacks, everything but leaves.
I find my clothes and wallet. My floor disobeys
when I tell it, *Stay beneath me.*
Lately an older man wearing
glasses and a robe peers out from behind a tropic-print
curtain, waiting for the chance to explain the meaning
and the spelling of his name.
He has three secrets he must split like logs,
each with ideas that curve down behind them in back,
each one leaving a sparkling green trail.
And then he shades off
into something relaxed and humane.

The Body of a Fish

Mother, may I touch your secret hand again
and tell you what I have been learning since you died?
The heart of a child beats here, in the chest
of a full grown man! There is no remedy for love.
No food, no drink, no drug or potion
can cure this sick heart's heaviness.
The jealous heart rejects all formulas
as truth stands before us, a store window
full of expensive goods we must carry.

You cannot regive me life that I may mar it again.
All your promises have become white fuzz
crackling in the bonfire of dreams, and those dreams,
those dreams! I cannot understand them,
their delights annoy me, their hopes sadden my heart.
The night leaves burn-marks on my bed.
I wish I had the body of a fish instead
of this ten-cent puddle of tears.

Following Mother Out of the Forest

An owl I didn't want to be flew away.
A brownstone I wanted to be lasted.
A bus whistled by. We no longer
cared who spoke. The air
felt charged with breath
we held back. A dark shape
slipped inside me and I spoke it.
I listened as a stone listens,
understanding nothing. My colors,
arbitrary, spun faster. *Mama,*
tell me not to come.
I came. Papa held a rare,
weak thing in his arms.
I thought of the smoke
from my one-way childhood
when I sat numb and thirsty,
Papa, come tell Mama.

Memory Kitchenette

On Sundays
our maple
syrup smiles back
from the ledge
of our world.

An occasional truck
hushes the black and white
feathery coughs
of our next door
neighbor's
bad dream.

Each speck of light's
a single prayer
that returns
in the form
of my father,
standing in the
moon's furry window,
peering from
the dusty robes
of apple blossoms.

Sleep-Away Camp

Father published a ghost story that
chirped in our pear tree every summer, all summer,
especially as dawn reached our bedroom windows
and we were most ourselves, whatever we were called.

Chirping in our pear tree every summer, all summer,
the story sang of Poe, August Derleth, Shirley Jackson.
We were most ourselves, whatever we called
each other or our story, which were almost the same thing.

Our story referenced Homer's nekuia and Mary Shelley's monster.
We couldn't help that we were raised as readers
of each other or our story, which were almost the same thing
as the earth with its tree and the summer-long chirping.

We couldn't help with that. We were raised as readers
and our childhood was a sky of authors, titles,
and the earth with its tree. The summer-long chirping,
a scarf for the wind, echoed as far as the river,

and our childhood was a sky. Full of authors and titles
as a big city library, we judged ourselves as misty and girlish.
A scarf made of wind echoed as far as the river,
leaving me starstruck, leaving you skeptical and sore.

At a big city library, we judged ourselves as misty and girlish,
but we found that sleepy, flawed judgment
had left me starstruck, had left you skeptical and sore.
When you found your true home, you went right to sleep.

You found sleep's flawed judgment,
its way of ending and beginning again, the alchemy of its storm.
You found your true home and went right to sleep
with only stars to watch you, and the marvelous river,

ending and beginning again like the alchemy of a storm,
especially as dawn reached our bedroom windows.
With only those stars to watch him, and the marvelous river,
father published that ghost story.

Tomorrow's Totems

I growled on the path
picked out for me, and my night vision
hid behind a soft gold veil.
I smelled my father's
freshly dug earth, knew
I needed room to breathe my own
bacteria, time to plan my back-story.

Many years passed. I sewed my plants
into an imaginary
kingdom of snow and feathers.
The forest failed.
Bitchy priests hummed carols only they know.

The clown I saw from a thousand yards waved his
aromatic panatela at the hawks circling his head.
The keys in his pocket were soul food.
His feet became
melons, his knees five-gallon containers.

I was a statue on the roof of your house. Tonight
we slip outside the manacles of our luck.
Do you hear the cries of the night birds?

"Yes, I hear them, and the prayer in them,
but my voice is tangled, and in love with all forgetting."

Life-Sized Cardboard Men

Like an idiot with a bag of treasure, the solstice moon spills everything. Mars gleams with an orange brown planetary light that looks great on you. Hold on to my arm – this may be the last time we speak.

Two years ago, I felt good. My mother and father had turned back into pieces of paper again. On my father's sugar farm, svelte athletes paraded in Day-Glo Spandex, startling their audiences with the depth of their sadness. I read Rexroth, Patchen, Oppen, McGrath, Spicer, Kaufmann, Meyers, and the figure of a man climbing a flight of stairs seemed to have been imprinted on each page of each volume.

Wandering through the neighborhood one afternoon, I came upon a rabbit in a bed of poison oak. A dozen little policemen came to hurry me away. Still, I kept yearning for a New York meal. My mismatched clothing surrounded me. Every morning, when I lay in my bed listening to trains, I thought their melody recapitulated the act of climbing the stairs to the top of the Tower of Babel.

The dry petals in your hand are the secret building blocks of the universe. What can we wear tomorrow other than leaves?

Mowing Song

When I was a child, nature gnawed me.
My father had rigged the mountains, and

careless stars tore holes in my parchment moon.
I slept until the summer afternoon.

September sun warmed my millennial roses.
My clock purred, I felt scaly, cool, and virgin.

I dreamed of egg-blood, hair ablaze.
An ergonomic body yelled "Mermaid! Come back!"

A Tiny Home-Made Milky Way

The little boy hiding in the coat closet
will never grow into his father's shoes.
The closet isn't a spaceship, and the overcoat
buttons aren't stars, just his
wakeful moments in the arms of a spell
that has now ended.

There is one earth, one moon. Oracles
point toward vaguely starlit landscapes where
fear of death awaits past rhubarb bushes,
down long, dried-out hills. He may go gently
to the land of capes and roses
where Hermes will be waiting with his section
of the quarrel between ancient and modern.

The boy wants what he wanted long ago
and you, over there, you say you want
to sleep with one woman every night,
and you, down here, you say you want to sleep alone?

Well, Father and Mother felt ambivalent, too.
I walk along the golden crust of the only
earth I ever believed in, cursing the fool
who invented the shovel,
                                        and there you stand
doubled over from laughing, talking about
a piece of fruit no one's allowed to touch.

Rereading Robert Hayden's "Those Winter Sundays"

I remember Sunday
morning shirt buttons
and shoes, and the rain that gave the world
an aroma of rainbows rubbed with tar. I remember
feeling like jays nested in their family tree, crackling
as children arranged their jacks beneath it.
I remember a walk past thousands of
solid citizens who had monkeys rolling inside them,
wanting to share the sunlight with those monkeys,
give the rest of the world's candy to the trees.

I wanted the sound of falling ice, rivers
in motion, healthy mallards
floating past thorn trees binding us to our fate.
I wanted teenage energy, perpetual
rhythms, undercurrents of October's
dreadful, burly beauty, which veils reason.
I wanted to tease darkness into greetings.

I built a better way, night by night,
out of the lumber of what
daylight left behind, heavy dry lumber
that burned a long time.

Frayed History

Dipped in a lake of hips and lawns,
collecting dew while studying jugglers,
I found a figure I liked, turned twelve under
wind and thunder, strings attached.
We spent afternoons reading their resonances,
nuances, and red deserts outside the periphery of these,
a magnetic blend of sky and sand tiptoeing past
our reading room. It all looked
back at us three times a day; we squirmed each time,
and called it prayer. My roughened skin had no place to land.

The wind chilled the wet grass slowly, and you went
outside to see it – now it all seems very small. On the
other side of the bent fence,
steel beasts, calm again, became the norm.
Girls in tight boat-neck
tees became our rearview mirrors. Night connected
people by striping the lights, white, then yellow.
Every lamp post cast its own.

We weren't animals despite the cages we lived in
or the snow-globes we kept trying to eat. We just remade
the larger gestures we'd observed
all our lives, a single hand-wave that proved
we no longer had to carry the sadder trajectory.
I must confide in you: my pillow
is full of bruised candy, my mattress is picked clean.

Our father has arrived in the form of an owl, and insists
he was the broken one, bright but forgotten
in the rush to the freeway entrance, too hurt
to give info, too badly burned to do more than keep his
head above water and give me my brown eyes.

The lights go out, he returns to the other world,
you hear the end of what the comedy is telling you.
The danger down there no man can describe.
I hear another story altogether, but I'm home.
You're a white streak inside a blue flame,
igniting a dark peak at the end of a black
road. I watch that streak again and again
drawing me deeper down into the place where you are.

Two Worlds

The pine trees are barely audible and no one
has translated the rocks. I think the chaparral
can say only phrases it picked up from wolves.
Before the revolution, every natural object had
a voice. Our wisest interpreted this miracle,
syllable by syllable, and that became our culture.

It lasted long enough to give way to other cultures
that sounded as if they spoke to no one.
The age of wonder and shared miracle
passed with the revolution, and the sighing chaparral
took over any authority our wisest ever had.
Even our dogs began acting like wolves.

But I had always felt an attraction to wolves;
I heard, in their midnight music, signs of a culture
I never imagined in animals. By fifteen, I had
intuited how wolf cries would sound in English. Telling no one
about this, I paced out in the chaparral,
frightened into silence by this miracle.

Everything I Touched

I arrived with a Muddy Waters LP and a typewriter.
Four years later I had an education
in how the sun worked the wind.
Strategy, pilots said.

I was the rambling kid, following a mandolin,
collecting errors. I cut up pages
of diaries where I recorded
lights on paths through forests.
The more doors I drifted
past, the prouder I grew. My pride
brandished teeth. My skin

obeyed the great mother no one
saw. I took walks with her ghost
to her house with a place for a horse
but before the horse came the man,
and she gave him lemons and pomegranates.
She signed my copy of her splendid book
and two engraved snakes hung over her door.

The Bedroom Which Is Also a Forest

I cantered off through an open meadow
toward an apple tree. The wind
was a drum that had lost its independence.
A single acorn begat a horizon – I could see its face,
it had been crying – the line was my mother and father,
and my heavy eyelids were shadows of her cool,
chestnut-colored hair. You emerged a hooded figure,
slamming doors, ringing blue diamond-shaped bells
that imprinted a single complex sentence on my memory,
one I've been trying to recreate tonight for you.
I'm trapped in this version of myself, you see,
these black-and-white hours of tease and flutter,
my pen has already been delivered
but my hand's too cramped and youthful to hold it
and when you tried to stop what I was doing
our reflection rose up from the mirror to the ceiling
and our dread became a comma between two distant purple trees.

The Frosted Code

I found our dream-nation's whole story the way you can sometimes see a whole tree in an acorn, or a whole basket of apples inside one spit-out seed. Faces of heroic men and admirable women from the late twentieth century started smearing and spinning like colored lights. Womanly hills held books open to my half-brother and me, so that we could read and learn the earthen forms of things we knew only from the Internet. And we did.

We ate baked sonnets and drank iced elegies out of tall glasses. Crimson-flecked leaves took on separate lives as they fell from their mother trees. A small disc of moonlight hinted at what careers we could expect. Not even our ignorance could have saved us from what had to happen.

Then I started a revolution with my half-brother – man, I wish we'd won. I wish I could tell you how cold the shears felt in our hands as we seized them, knowing the crimes that filled our hearts would put us in prison for life... cold and hard as the hand of God.

Now the pig-slop the cops call "rain" has stopped, my fingers have turned to pointed sticks, and wherever I gesture with my alien fist, soldiers and students out-shout me, and my faith turns into a mood. The sun burns off the morning haze and threads late-summer light through the trees. We have oars we must insert into our whirlpools of punishment and consolation, changes we must make in each other's ideas of love.

The goal is depth, not breadth. All those whom we admire have gone deep into their wells, and now our hour has come; we must dismantle our scripts and enter our dark, repellant well, without mentors, doctrine, or flashlight. The reward comes later, and it's easy to miss.

The problem was not in our upbringing. Our mother was kind and filled with mercy, our father was just and knew the ways of men; our aunts and uncles offered us food and comfort. The voice of the family rides a horse, but the horse is not made of words.

Right away, we recognize our problem and the veiled dream-knowledge that leads us toward it, then away. There was, it turned out, a perfect place for us, but once we found it we had run out of things to say to one another, and stood out in the soft rain with the part of ourselves that gives itself to language, undernourished and misshapen, but nonetheless real.

"Live erect, and unspool what you know": a noble commandment. Oh, my moonlight-speckled city, I could give accounts of so many things! But I can only instruct mythological animals how to talk to salesmen, how to use the Spanish of water and hands!

Reunion

The coach bid farewell, and the headmaster smooched
his teary wife at the banquet table.
Other flaws displayed themselves openly, badly;
a few even had names. They do that all the time now
at the old place – you know, the one where
that sameness hangs over the tops of gardens
each evening? Fourteen years somehow pass
and dry leaves hang like punctuation from the branches.

We got a happy ending when folk specialists
endorsed its cool, uncomfortable pond. One painter
left for Mexico and wanted a pie mailed to her there.
I told her "the world's an inaudible audience,
and in its last soft moments it froths up, like
tide-foam when a wave pulls out."

Supper Club Cubism

Needing a break from *Scarface*, I opened an art history textbook and started coloring the black and white plates with Sharpies. You glanced at the collection our father willed us and spat. A cell phone chimed. You liked my Sharpie style and so did I after you said you did.

We both heard a slanting voice grumble from the shed in back of the house. The voice may have been a man, may have been a goat – the way the voice sounded, it could have been some blend of both – and what he said, when we heard it clearly, became a hand, a cool hand to reformat our brows.

He told us we had to wade through ten fields shit to find one ounce gold. He warned us about how the past goes on glowing. He warned us too about how we could turn into used-up angels, reciting old poetry to rooms of restless accountants. He left us with one command: "On a silent, dove-gray pavement slab you'll find a slip of paper. Stop, read it and continue walking toward the triple crossroad, one block north of here."

In our earlier life, we'd stood in silence when a slain man's son returned to see the house where his father died. He cried out loud, and we listened. I'm thinking about his grief. It was not something we had to pity. It was something we simply had to hear.

In this life, if I keep focused on the slip of paper, I'll get off that dove-gray slab, find the key that opens the saltbox house, and cherry-pick whatever may still wait there. But a gust of wind pulls the slip of paper from my hand, and it glows harder the tinier it gets.

The Gear that Turns the Sky

How sweet, to shrug off childhood,
to bid farewell to the heroes who

botched it! I slipped off the world I used to wear
and everything I saw had edges and outlines,

colors all their own: red clay, cranberry, cut grass.
The sky's unlimited, yet striped with tape.

This morning I passed judgment on
the moon, a tiny crescent in a late spring sky.

You said I was made of magnesium
and boxer shorts. I hid my

kewpie face behind a volume of Emerson.
No one can explain why or how these mornings

take the form of a path made of shoes leading up a hill,
each shoe recalling a suffering face, wide with grief

or dead, mummified in that scream-face position
while other fruits and flowers begin a long, glum fade.

In the Shadow of a Slice of Birthday Cake

Yes, say the elders, it is good to have an older brother, one whose wing you feel cool and strong beneath, for an older brother is an image of the future. Oh, it is good to hear the call of the past, to heed that voice; it is good to re-cry tears we shed when our losses were fresh, and to re-laugh at what once made us lighthearted. Yet it is also good to see an image of one's possible destiny, and so it is good to have an older brother, or one who serves that duty.

I was fifteen years old, full of how wind falls onto trees and sets loose pods and pebbles of memory, scented with eucalyptus dust, or dusted with eucalyptus scent, whichever it is. Nothing yet had been heard from the night. I wasn't implicated in any of it. I simply ate my macaroni and read *Ramparts*. No one hurried to save me from anything that went bump or yanked the moneychain.

She felt ambivalent. Ceilings seemed lower, and while the idea of many small rooms wasn't fundamentally objectionable, these rooms were like storage boxes with connecting aisles, and you were supposed to live and sleep in these boxes, getting from one to another through a system of stairs and catwalks. This is going to take some getting used to, she said to herself, as she lay down next to the coffee maker. But another scary dream shook her awake at 4:15 am, and her hands trembled as she lit a cigarette and heated milk in a pan.

I remember standing in a dingy wind, looking at the city full of men in black leather and women in red lipstick and tight short dresses, then walking to the lip of the freeway and sticking out my thumb. Night opened its hermaphroditic thighs, which no one can look upon for long – that's why it grows dark – and somewhere a bard began his heroic song.

I heard the bard's voice as though it came from my own interior, and suddenly raw material of all kinds started pouring out of every socket, speaker, screen, page, and mouth. Onstage, actors sucked sugarless fruit-flavored hard candy, and played out their characters' sour, Rube Goldbergish lives. The set design recalled William Steinberg's fineness of line and offered cryptic explanations of what was supposed to make the cat push the tennis ball onto the bird nest, etc., written in an epigrammatic, syntactically puzzling style too close and too far off to be readable, too important and too trivial to comment upon.

The scene began with wagging fingers and gnomes, fairies, elves and all of that group hopping in zany motion through green pastures, sheep shit, all that. Then a tragic hand dropped coffee onto the backs of the assembled like a thunderstorm, and humid electric cling fueled up the air like reggae.

I didn't get it at first. An overweight man wearing only a red G-string explained my noncomprehension to me as a consequence of insufficient cream in my diet. "You must drink more cream," he said, through his red-and-gray Van Dyke beard. I suddenly felt able to fly. I looked at the face of my old-fashioned watch. The crystal shaped itself into a lens.

I looked through and saw the same man stride confidently across a stage to a piano, sit and begin an Ellington medley. Some stared at his G-string, some at his beard; others simply dismantled their salads. I stretched my legs, my neck, even my fingers, but still heard, even above the piano music, the crackling sound of spring, landing on the roof with heavy, booted feet.

She remembered lying in bed at night alone, half awake, the day's events turning in her mind, fire-tails from falling stars visible enough to wish on. The creamy sound of trumpets and trombones guarded the images at the center of her wishes, inchoate though they may have been. Some part of them may have come true. Now, she wonders, was she misleading herself all along? Everyone she knows smells of dark roasted coffee and lemon cake every time – the predictability's wearing her out. If only someone smelled really, really bad!

Yes, say the elders, it is good for the young to act foolishly, that they may demonstrate the truth of the proverb and thereby earn the right to learn its wisdom. It is good that kinetic moments be preserved in all their explosive immediacy, so that we may come to love their power to frighten and liberate, thrill and heal. It is good to look into a tiger's eye, fill a truck with your belongings, drive it to a place you've never been, and build a new life there. How much of the world's great story moves in just this way, through the foolish beauty of the heart!

Entering the Maze

The ones who raised us had vanished. Our lives
were as real as they would ever be,
and midway through side four
in the double-album of our innocence
we packed an overnight bag and headed to our favorite city.

There, we saw cats in trees, dogs falling from ledges,
and a river that gathered pictures of beauty and death
carried us past smoking landscapes
tufted with spray.
Our whirling panic tasted like
a chain. At interviews, our faces
were miniature cannon in a Civil War specialty store window.
Our first jobs lasted ten and eleven months, yours in night court
typing pleas, mine in a boatyard inspecting yachts.

We saw lights at the end of our grindstones, but
something underground had happened. The huge world
opened its scented home, invited us in for a sip.
Our ideals set giants loose in the ether, and
canceled all returns to the mainland. We repeated
prayers, opened windows, and released birds
into the curry-scented night.

A Hand Slipping from Behind a Cloud

Everything felt magnified, tilted in
inviting ways I didn't want to correct.
How far was I from home? Who cared? This day
held a gift for me, and I could feel it in my hand.
The field in back of my mind was never so fully lit,
and my deformed but lovable heart no longer shied away from
the force of that light. We had been spending our summer
afternoons in reference stacks. Now, we faced an
October sun, and our eyes widened at its gleam
as though a songbird waited inside it, to be set free
into branches of wood and leaves of fire. My companion
and I had only to munch at our options to raise brand-new
cathedral-sized doubts. But as the roses withered, and their
petals fell, we remembered the pointless
luxury of kissing the grass. Back at the library,
an invisible worm had found a home
in an old medical dictionary on the top shelf,
and the sun bluffed its way through
the equinox undisturbed. The light had an idea.
It broke through our window and felt proud of itself, yet
there were things it could not have known
about our sprees, and how we stumbled into chasms.
When love sours, the world releases dust into
our eyes, and the lover becomes a drunk
who reveals only family secrets.
We drew no distinctions between the mind and
the sea; we washed our feet and ankles, and as
the water's surface broke, we saw semblances of plot,
with a tree going mad in the late August wind.

I pulled myself from the place you call my home,
remembering dishes, flower petals, cancelled
foreign stamps I loved so much as a boy in
uniform, marching through the soft darkness, but a wet light
lurked around thorn bushes, showing me an image

of joys I lost when we parted. Nights
drifted down the mountain like warm palms made to hold
my jaw. Dust revealed textures we misread.
Our hands were now those of a stranger, sliding past
the spines of shiny, thin books, stopping only
to pluck one string, then gone in search of
a reservoir. My hands shook as they offered their gift,
a drifting, smoky thing that brought no birds.
Autumn was a porcupine, scattering hubbub through
the streets of old town, and the animal's pale
needles got all bunched together, so
I winnowed them with my hands; as I did,
I talked to myself about everything and nothing,
ran fingers across my scalp and saw words like flat stones
skip across a pond, mad as a devil. With a
blank look, I pretended to be happy, and ate
what lay on my plate. When I untied my wagon,
I suddenly saw what looked like you in a stream, holding
a "Repent" sign. Good thing we'd ordered French fries,
hot and crisp, with chili and garlic. But could we have ever
learned vastness? Streams of time trembled and barked,
a weak wind scattered ripples across soft, unrefined earth.
Where had the steel lions gone? Life told a story of
beauty and fear, but no one, we learned later,
had heard of the book in the hero's hand.
His life was a finger sandwich, a slick surface with
a concealed nozzle that squirts a wonderful croon
over your birthday cake. Spoiler alert: he ends up
in a river, on his way to the sea, holding nothing.

Three decades before all this, I came, carrying
other books; you had left your door open a crack, and
I exhaled loud enough to awaken birds from their foliage.
I'm still trying to decipher their cries. I know they call me
toward deeper waters, away from neat rows,

and wiggle as the sun sinks behind its redwood world,
eager for penance. Meanwhile, a Santa Ana wind
lifts your hair. Further west, a knitted towel
waits for your wet shoulders at the end
of a pathway made of starlit clouds. When the violent
songbirds argue, we hear how weak they really are
yet they fly past servant and master, genius and idiot,
and make phrases we still can't quite find inside ourselves.
A drunken sadness inhabits this dark forest, and
sucks the error from our words. Our particular
experience, not anyone else's, concerns us now.
Those phrases made in haste and dropped carelessly
along the path to the lake are dust now, but above us,
branches still hold to their mother trees. We sail
a small vessel across a lake, scared in our white jeans,
adoring the bowl of night, how red it turns, how dense.
Its face has jewels for eyes. When our irises match,
which happens twice a day, my desk starts buzzing,
the glass in my window remembers heat and sand.
What still puzzled me takes the form of two soft
hedges: one hides a message, the other simply
offers shade. I kissed you first,
and we invented equations with our fingerprints
and blanket, not knowing what sort of luck
would rub us. We could have predicted
blank looks from the inner circle, but not
the sweet aroma they left when their simple story
turned toward us and begged us to carry its burden,
savor its lessons, and stand alone.

The Little Figured Box We Dreamt About Has Been Returned

My calendar never had so many days to spare – so many, I could have given them away to beggars, stubbed them out in ashtrays, recycled them like cans – and all our big ideas were just taking shape. The clock read only quarter of three; the young, supple afternoon had hours left to present its ripening, its dissolution into evening, its cooling into night.

Pomegranates symbolized only the teeth-marked hearts of sad lovers, and the seeds of one peppered your dull patchy lawn with red dots. Most of the town's apples had also started to glow.

Some wild-animal quality in your demeanor, the way you occupied space as you sat in a chair, convinced me to trust you. Your face looked selected by some infallible judge.

Under your bed, you kept a monster for warmth and protection. The monster disregarded my attempts to win his friendship as consistently as Penelope disregarded her hundred-fifty-seven suitors. I heard it cough and turn as I tried to sleep next to you. "You're the salt on my beans," I told it, "the pepper on my rib." Hidden behind what I wanted to say, I rose happily from bed, my heart a distant blue beacon.

I see that whole period now in the way one sees the shape of a work of art: in a sudden "aha!" moment, akin to paranoia yet benign, with delighted wonderment in place of fear: Innocence, not Experience; the Lamb, not the Tyger. Look, for example, at this slide. Here we come in our disgusting burnt-orange 1981 AMC Gremlin, wanting what we cannot have. *I know what I like to hold*, I said. And I held it; infancy returned like the sun; I wept and hated my fruitless weeping, then asked myself,

“If, as a man tosses a rock, he hears a voice inside him saying, ‘The path this rock will follow is a metaphor for your future life. If it rolls only a short while, your life will be short; if it bounces against other rocks, your life will collide with others’ lives; where it comes to rest, there will you rest,’ ought we to applaud him for his openness to metaphor, or pity his childish willingness to accept on faith the most arbitrary impositions?”

We were waiting for a signal to arrive like a gift, but what we thought no longer mattered. We had no credible ideals, and the screen presented people from random times and cultures, like the Fates. You remember the Fates: Clotho spins the fabric of life, Lachesis measures its length, Atropos cuts the thread, and a tragic moustache rows a tiny boat across my kitchen counter.

An Era Like Ours

There's a naked child in the pasture, and the wind knows his time.

He learns to live among strangers and their gravel; mired in the forest of their dust, he leaves when spring brings green. The road becomes a snake who knows what he means. He scrapes each bowl and corner clean, but the fire god reveres chaos and slaps his impeccably calm cheek. His hand pivots, prying open sad dreams.

On the day after Groundhog Day, a small crowd gathers at the Grange Hall to hear the Coastal Valley Brass Band play its annual fundraiser. Waffles are always served. I look into a ceiling of fluorescent tubes and he stares back, reaches down and pulls tangerines out of my mouth, one after another, without stopping.

He causes cherry trees to grow, and ties them with straps that resemble my teenage years.

I laughed; the fire god had just slapped you, too, and you stood on the froth of a wave like Aphrodite, shining through pages of a cheaply printed Bible, lovely as shaking dew. Your chirping friends could be heard all over the Web.

The Twelve Original Beatles Albums

I am the one who asks you to ask me why.
I am fourteen years old; six of those years were written by others.
I am never tired of pleasing you, although
I am getting ready to tell you my secret:
I am born the day Sylvia Plath dies.

I am christened the day John Kennedy dies.
I am, in all seasons, only halfway visible.
I am just about to change the way you see yourself.
I am sending something very close and hot to you.
I am sitting alone, like you, in a bedroom.

I am a part of a large, well-loved black-&-white picture
made of many tiny black-&-white pictures.
I am leaping, running, jumping, but always pursued.
I am thirteen years old, and all those years are mine.
I am the only one in my class.

I am, as my face shows, winning this big, fast game, but
I am, and have always been, a loser in the small, deep game.
I am pledged to make no reply to that question.
I was worried when my darling began wearing black.
I am still worried, so I look back into the German past.

I am now so worried I make my worry a comedy.
I am hiding my mother's body under a pair of flutes.
I am holding someone's ticket, someone who does not care what
I am about to lose, and that ticket admits one person.
I am one of over sixty thousand, but I am still alone.

I am not cute anymore, according to my new friend.
I am standing in one of my gardens, and I swear,
I am not looking at what I ever saw before.
I am making no plans in the normal sense.
I am so moved by beauty that I start speaking French.

I am going to the graveyard with a notebook and a melody.
I am switching my left and right hands for the sake of satire.
I am dressed in frightening black-&-white, but
I am still the most colorful day in August.
I am ending an important part of your life.

I am changing my name and surrounding myself with ghosts.
I am the result of an unexpectedly boring process.
I am a sketch for a picture that no one ever painted.
I am, nevertheless, everybody's favorite favorite.
I am never goosing you any other way.

I am an accident that turned out better than well.
I am American, for the first and last time.
I am a bus chartered by a fool and a blue jay.
I am flying on my lifted-up heart – and look! There
I am in front of the world with gum in my mouth.

I am still in a funk from a month of spiced peas, and
I am still mourning a man who had secrets.
I am not guilty, but I keep that to myself.
I am thirty years old, and every year shows what I hid.
I am packed with gifts you hung on your walls.

I am walking across a street on an August afternoon.
I am thinking about Her Majesty, The Queen.
I am, even for those who eat me, only half a loaf.
I am the last movement of an act of love that
I am still the start and symbol of.

I am the last, or am I the next-to-last? I know
I am part of a sad, broken, garish thing.
I am ambivalent about where I fit here. But
I am glad I mentioned trains, ponies, our hard year.
I am – oh, the luck! – framed on both sides by deep black.

Poem Wearing Feathers We Picked from the Ground

Our childhood books, stacked and shelved,
blocked a twinkling crimson light
and we checked the wind, which was an old man.

We never stopped falling, the ducks never quit
their dark pond, the train was our two bodies
imagined as one, passing in a haze.

The steady sun's a beacon, boys, we're bound for better weather.
"This coconut represents our planet. When we use tools,
it comes to life."

The sun skidded. We counted the hours it missed,
their long rumbling hours of seduction, their
secretly selected trees.

My left arm watched the ocean open its window
one summer night, and my right arm parked
itself, listening to its breeze.

Both horrible and not, the summer leaves my
family name in the book of the missing,
not the book of burnt cream.

I come back to you, every year, wearing my
name around my neck, never letting go of
my bird in my cage.

Tonight strikes me as composed,
not informed. We're dancing like *Peanuts* characters
with grown-up emotions.

I find my home temper strange and hard.
The sun, marinated in fog and dust,
gives light to both full and empty.

We cannot linger on the question of shoes
and sidewalks, for a single leaf will fall from its tree
and land no matter our answer to it.

The slow, hushed turn of the year sees its lessons
in the form of a secret ball we hold as
we enter the winter's ropey mouth.

I wish the light had been shaded by thoughts
that change color, as if the mind were made
of irises wild as dust.

Outside my window, someone has laid
a blanket, and sits on it now, staring at
the place where the sky began.

Sonnet

Shall we win at love? Shall we lose? We meant no harm.
We kept rags for our wonderful pleasures,
we counted on disciplined sheep. Grainy love-cradles
landed on the anguished floors of our earth.

If a woman cries and is not heard, there was no grief,
no begging for blossoms, no searing scarlet angels.
The shape of night smuggles in the hardness of silent things.

The man looks up at her shoe, remembering the lies he told.
He is an erotic coward, promising a crescent moon and an echo.
The night drags them both along like a single unit
of meaning, and everything they lose laments.

We whispered yesses to each other, remembering
how resilient we always wanted to be.
In the morning, we faced another unemployable deity.

Many Pairs of Eyes

At the beginning, I was a human salad, a crisp, dew-spotted witness to a new blank space where someone before me had worked out an agreement I was now in the process of enacting. Fear and freedom, uneasy brothers, opened a restaurant/bar in my chest.

By the midpoint, I was seated on a hard chair. The kitchen had a few more people in it, and we got along fine. The spring afternoon warmed our faces and chests, and the future made me smile. My friend came by the next afternoon with a fifth of gin. It was only a few minutes past five; the day was starting to dissolve into dark blue shadows and silhouetted trees. I heard horses talk among each other, sharing their lengthy memory. Violins played soft gospel tunes an acre away.

Suddenly, the feeling of the early 1960s freshened the air (President Kennedy, the Mercury astronauts, *James Brown Live at the Apollo*), suggesting that nothing familiar would exist much longer. A force pushed outward from my chest and shoulders like rivers offering lessons I remembered from trees and the winding path toward the bridges between them.

I had no secrets anymore. Once it seemed I had a million, but they all leaked out, dampening my pages as they came out from the upstairs windows and landed over the nearby fruit trees (they help keep them warm, too, for winter lies severe upon us now, winter and its temptations to burrow and to hoard). Hence my retreat to my mountaintop cabin where I may pass the rest of the evening with you, by a fire, while winter descends around us.

Look at the rice on my plate: speckles of light. The coffee waits in its cup like a burrowed animal. A pincushion, a matchbox from a Sag Harbor bar, a copper postcard and a piece of cactus candy lie secure inside a cigar box, waiting for someone to read what they spell out.

Another Shapely Evening

My heart grew up inside an echo chamber
where rockets took off and landed on giant, four-letter words.
Palm-prints lay deep in the mind, and never eroded.
With a candle, I could see the bones in your hands.

The land looked vast.
Behind its veil, a herd of young men saying *Maybe* to each other
started falling into their private worlds.
We ate our sluggish dinner. Music began,

low and hushed,
a slow march-tune building until we felt carried off
to an unknown destination inside us.

By now, we have reached that place.
No wonder you shield your face from me.
Creamy petals scatter onto the shoulders of the seraphim
like a matinee made of glass.

Fallen Angels

In private, I was fruitful. You were a snake on a raft,
hiding from shamans who would grab you for
a ritual. Drumbeats echoed from the shore,
congas, bongos, shakers...

The neon janitor bore it away.
In the discreet morning, we awoke blameless,
our dignity moving like a ship.
We saw no gap-years,
no do-overs,
no faces that could help a toddler walk across a pond.

We were even-Steven in the empty afternoon, nibbling
at sandwiches, grateful to breathe.
It was a method,
or a diagram of one. Angels sat with us for
ten-minute sessions and worked out whatever
distracted us from the greater business of
living. Sadness fogged
over every spring afternoon and stayed with us like the need
for water. We paid our bills with our hair.

I got off the train at a little coastal town
and made my noir life out of fog and my cells. Petunia
days were behind me. My beginner status sat there,
came unsealed
and stopped fighting fair. The
landscape tempted us to scrape moss
from a boulder, but it wasn't the central problem:

I looked around but all I saw
was a champion lunch-box man
whose grip assured you what we had was really love. As we
read in silence, a small child placed a bucket on my head.

Whispering Objects

I had become a rumor. Near my bed, a book
lay open to one special page. I left a light for you
and your burden. You'll see it when the time is right.

You'll see it, and I'll know it, but we cannot
name or describe it, and we who have grown up into it
learn to hide inside it. Only our feet keep us human.
Our chanting voices carve air into numbers, and
a hundred clouds have encircled the moon by now.

That means tonight, on our cloud, we take
a test together, looking down with longing
at ripples on the surface of a long, secret lake.

Everything Trembling

I looked in my purple-tinted mirror,
scooped up my footprints
and got ready for the roads.

No animal knew my name, no wild plant told me its secrets.
I made my way along the edges of many brooks
but the images came blurry, their faces far away.

At such moments, your sort of face
turns east. The map of veins we carry on our hands
directs us to this moment of charity, or clarity.
A cowboy's hammer amplifies the wind.
Twilight gets bluer and saltier when we sit together
in it, teens again, plugged into the air.

From my jacket dangles a barn covered with snow.
Its door opens to a night that whirls and slumps,
running with rain and telling our friends how
I bend over you to grow money in your dreams.

Birthday Curse

This isn't a story about potatoes or meat.
It's about how we didn't notice the summer afternoon
bearing down on the slightly sloping hill
until it faded out the redness of our story,
the part where we first fell naked onto
a mountain of paper napkins.
I think how lucky I was at that moment.
When the scene turned oppressive, I had smart
exit lines and a pot of black beans
simmering nearby, like a fool.

I have the fountain pen I used that night – it still writes.
This story is kind of about it,
more than it is about its characters or the new
century that offered us its cupped hand like a confidant.

You sip what looks like water
and white lights stir in your glass.
Our son, too young to drive through
the fine print of his living, polishes
his buckle and wonders.

Would you like to help me pick up a few things
around here? The sun's still banked behind a blurry,
ash-colored cloud, so comforting, so encouraging of order.
My economy starts early and looks glad to see me.
I suck, too, sometimes. It's only fair.

I Looked Up

My shoes couldn't
reject the magnetized
road. I traveled like
a kiss calling to
a barely seen window. Then
I connected my idea of heaven
to a rose, whose mark
is a scent, or a nested
jay yelling *I am* to vines,
gulping down the day. Shadows
abounded, buried in print.
Even the shyest animals
climbed downstairs to smell
visitors through the window.
The future crisped us with its
clothes, dirty, stylish.
Before going back to sleep
each day filled one box
with its name. I looked
up like any soldier
but war stayed way down below, with
the moon, who begged like a pro.
I swallowed my milk and felt
better. I blinked as though
the world were snow.

Evening in the Valley

The moon tonight looks
planted, like public art.
We know why we sit here.
Orange dusk, an elaborate
chocolate Easter egg,
coffee: the scene, a plump
waterfall, stays with us
behind the stand of oaks.
The scene's a single piece
where your mother's
a wooden spoon, stretching
its arm in front of the sun,
and your father's a big

model airplane hanging
from a ceiling, and
a question about the world
and space underneath it starts
to flood it, it seeps through and
he is helpless against this
water now, he faces his
fluorescent ceiling with closed
eyes and waits for the flood-tide
to ebb. This is his only way.

Will he let me continue. My right
arm, lazy animist, feels big
and curious. I cover it with
a shirt sleeve, white, and
stand apart from it. For the gods,
time needs thorough explanation.
Even afterwards, they don't
get it. So I dug in the overgrown
woods, remembering doors
that would not let me out,

days my father looked at
his broken bucket and swore,
for that was his only way.

In a background, I tried pleasing
them all. I was a seventeen-year-old
cupboard, grinning, lemon-scented,
holding onto a handful of rain
water. I remember your father
again, looking up and waiting,
even now. I never knew him.
I never knew your mother, either.
I understand she would sing as
she prayed, and made great latkes.
The dusk has emboldened the trees
into saying "yes" to our question.

The Unfolding

The winter left cuts on everyone's hands, cobwebs in
every bedroom corner. I watched the sunset from a bus.
Those around me watched it through their bandaged hands,
and they held spoons in their mouths, every one of them.
My neck muscles opened like a wall calendar.
Out on the street, winter reminded everyone to relax.

The woman who invented the human voice
also invented the finish line.
Hers is a voice I know in my sleep.
I'm scared of it, specifically of being turned
down a trail that made up a life
to be read from bottom to top like the Ching.

I thought back to Wednesday, but the mechanism
shined too brightly, then the focus
shifted to a scene I wasn't in.
I closed my eyes. The moon shed its scarves
over the confused, the frightened, the under-prepared.
In the smooth piece of land behind my brows,
a little man finished sketching his perfect piñata.
I looked up and asked my hero to explain.

The Fortune Teller's Palm

Spring rain lifts
and tones the scene:
arthritic sycamores,
pewter-colored and out of reach,
flaunt delicate, glossy
pains. I place a chocolate
cherry in my mouth, hold it
ten seconds before biting down.

I understand my heroes
better than ever; their
courage stands sprinkled
with lemon. But
tell me this, you who claim
to know nothing but love,
why must the monkey in me growl?
I say, you will take a long and complex journey
into the pines that wait outside your dining room.
Their roots go deep in your chest and hips.
The stars will pass overhead slowly as canoes.

I need salt and an orchid blossom to endure
another ten minutes of this silence.

The Night Mouth

The full moon last night witnessed everything we
laughed at and stretched. We walked among water-lilies,
wearing our mantles, feeling that we lived in some verdant
primal forest among fields of heather. A pouch
of rhinestones fell open, strewing violet light across
even the cheapest version of ourselves. I should have
removed my mask much earlier, but that steady stream of
mud left me short on fight, so I stayed inside my smiling cloud
like a shy prayer, dusted myself, and admitted that
everything I wanted had a double meaning, and a compliant fire
at its center, a fire that remembered some things.

I wonder how those who never played hide-and-seek
learned my name. I'm here on a whim, holding a limbo stick
in one hand, a lucky coin in the other, standing near this place
of departure where I feel the water calling to me,
inviting me to travel by sea to distant places, and soon
we're floating along in the best paradox ever built, with
a warm bottle at the foot of our bed, and a sky outside
that bleeds as it marches past our ship the way I once
drove past billboards advertising coats made from the
shimmering golden fur of enormous, rare beasts.

Our history's unique, though, and indigo to the core.
My arms prop up a future mother and father, both asleep.
Storm clouds grow bigger and darker. What, besides
this, do I need to know? If I lose my balance, the ship
disappears, and I come to in a forest where muscled hands
clench in sympathy with the voice of my father, which tumbles
in indictment of this landscape's race-car red flower beds where
one finds every year of the recent past – the ebony
striped ones, pale yellow ones, even ones that sing
in chorus at moments of crisis, when our story turns,
and rests his head.

Responsible Adults

She is still asleep. Yet her bed lies next to our grandfather's clock, which chimes loudly every fifteen minutes and booms for more than a minute every hour. Cows low and sway under her open window, and one young man (he looks like the young Fred Astaire, overwhelmed by longing) is duking it out with her uncle out back by the well while frightened chickens run back and forth.

The rain stops very slowly, and a wretched moon keeps silence as it shines down on the blue hoods of SUVs sleeping in driveways. Cupid's arrow just hit me again, but I refused to hold hands with my guardian angel, despite the holes remaining in his heart. Yet the cold night air fills with the sense of our having been exempted from some terrible tax or other kind of great reckoning. *They know all about you*, the air seems to say, *but they're letting you live anyway.*

December comes twice a year now, once as a plant, once as an earthworm. This time, people were trying a modified solar-myth approach to financial and workplace issues. You liked summer best, so you acquiesced. Earth ground up the struggle to act elegant and you tried not to laugh out loud at the air. I kept my nose clean and figured out ways to cut back through the old neighborhood into the snowy part of someone's woods.

Dazed young engineering students walked slowly past displays of fine crystal goblets and polished silver dishes, blinking at the wattage. Angels of rerun and farewell flew high above the stars, waves took whole neighborhoods into the sea, and everyone seemed to have that monitored look – and oh, that ring around the moon...

Let's not sentimentalize primitivism, though – I looked up authority in a number of books, got shocked by the prices, checked my rights at The Law Store and voted. Boy, what a surprise! My candidate glimpsed a Manx napping on a laptop and took cheer from that, so what the hey. He was driving a jazz guy's Cutlass and his money was clearing up, like a nose. And the wallpaper: each Tenniel *Alice in Wonderland* illustration was given its own little space.

She is still asleep. A warm light seems to hang a few feet above her – is it an illusion, suggested by the lateness of the hour? Prickly, ripe, shaky, complex, full of cracks, Mother Earth opens herself, but not for our comfort. We lie in our red sheets and look at the glare from the street and cannot ask each other a single question. I'm a responsible adult now, with a pair of tin cans tied to the end of my name! The vast warm darkness...

And then I deliver my notes to the neighbors and everything looks peachy again.

In Another Dance

The last three men I met all told me
the ocean is the world's real body.
One man gave me a ball
of rubber bands, the kind from
the 99-cent store. It heated up my palm
until I let it go, and I'll tell you
what else he told me:
"We are nothing but clouds of mud and lust."

The blue hills have leached all kleos from the sky.
The mouse scurries at the owl's hoot,
oak trees give us quiet wooden gifts.
Thick fog rests on the hills, erasing them. No
bristles spoil the pearl view of our cottage,
no one registers surprise.
My vision's muddy and speckled
but behind the curtain, I can make out my enlarged thumb
wiping my stubborn, enlarged lips.

We geared our lives toward fields lined with trees,
fields with places for fires and tents.
If birds wept, we didn't hear them – we had
just enough moonlight to find our blankets and flashlights.
We would settle in with Volume Two of something
and forget when we fell asleep, spooning together for
warmth. The sun in our faces woke our itching bodies.
I studied a single fallen leaf, found nothing to denounce,
or spill.

We preferred a world we understood, where wheels
turned calmly, and the natural blank check we get at birth
awaits its compassionate pen. These dreams, I have no
reason to doubt, caught us in a hug and shouldered us
into the cashmere voices we use with the women we meet.
I remember mouthing "OK" to you as the light

changed everyone's skin to something less white.
The modern language.

I pour us another coffee. Who's the angel at the bottom of my cup,
breast-stroking through the summer afternoon? Did he jump?
Did he fall? Was he pushed? Soon stars begin
staging their gradual entry, and day turns back,
away from us, toward somewhere else. The boy I was
has broken into tiny smiles.

I turned around to check our dashboard compass and felt
the air turn scarlet, scented with unseen pines.
I put away the guidebook – it wasn't written with coyotes
in mind – and opened a blank notebook. The ground was suddenly
splattered with colored light. A few minutes later,
my smart-aleck doppelganger implored the concierge
to let me sleep in the lobby, where at least there were
real people, not these phantoms. And one woman, suddenly
smiling back at us, removed her dark glasses as evening
fell. The string tied around her right index finger
confused me. When I touched the string, it
grew brittle, and snapped. But I made money off it
anyway, since it reminded so many customers of their younger
selves, when they could have "gone pro" at – what was it,
skipping stones across a pond?

All we could do, we had already done, and
all our fears turned into the memory of rain.
I suppose it helped us see how fully we live in
ritual, and how much like missiles we are becoming, in
our tolerance for doom. A ceremony was already beginning
that involved our feet, and breaking bread.
I threw the Ching just after you left for work this morning:
earth, overlooking a lake, observes the approach of a man
with three mouths. Yes, I see him too, driving north,

clouds mirrored by his shiny car beneath them,
a party of clouds rocking themselves into wisps.
I sat out in a meadow yesterday, listening to the summer
wind giggle and squeal at me. My water-bottle was my
companion, better than a dog. I forced myself to
recognize the pattern, or a token of the pattern,
but I had to "become" the pattern in the way a field of weeds
"becomes" a pattern when the wind puts its hands on it,
hushing and impressing.

Different plans were being made for you and me.
The tempo of the jazz sped up, roses got
bigger and fierier, pieces of old fence wood
dropped onto the earth. I placed my fingertips on your cool back,
took your hand. Your dress was a tulip. The crisp petals swerved
and curled like arrows, or a bird headed toward a large white cloud,
and a grin got systematic all over my face
and chest, as though I'd crossed three people's yards
to get here on time but the clock was moving at three
different speeds at once and huge clouds cover every
star anyway.

We live in a period short on forgiveness, and angry cacti
have started growing in my bedroom like tales from
the distant past. How quickly lucid dreams turn to water-stains!
I was a child on a green lawn, watching from below
as the refrigerator door opened, and the light from inside
blended with the earth.

And then, the great hiding began, and our lives took place
more and more slowly, as in a performance whose
reds and yellows drew the eye away from us in our off-white
robes, standing far away on the high-breasted hills
where thorny branches made dire patterns for us, a gift so pure
we still cannot interpret it.

I hadn't touched my flute in a year, my hammer and saw in
longer than that. The situation had straight and crooked
paths, and I repeated their names to myself to know
their histories. Instincts told us to get quiet and listen,
then decide whether the stars were shining
sarcastically down at us, and what the winds were begging us
to do for them. And then, we put on our thick black mittens and
painted a grid over it.

Later, after we'd completed school and lost our first jobs, we
gathered at the bar of the Disneyland Hotel and tried comparing
definitions of *noir*. I looked through the nearest window at the
parking lot, where the dullest part of our childhood was magnified
into a postulate. Dust-devils threw leaves at cars, and the leaves
kept moving, kept falling, kept yearning for slumber, aching for it,
and I felt and ached with them.

By now, the solid ground had traded places with a watercolor
of itself. Any enquiries were met with a sales pitch,
silky-smooth and piney as Christmas, and midway through it,
you'd notice leaves had started to grow spots, and the air
began tasting warm and leafy.
The moon looked deep, rambunctious, even,
so we praised the finches glowing in its light,
scattered clouds behind rustling branches,
yellow, or white, or faded green.
They were the visual equivalent of sugar, staining and
crusting our mouths when we tried eating it out of the box,
crinkling up and landing as gently as my tongue
lands in your mouth. The moonlight rushed from field
to field. The shore shimmered as it changed size. It felt
as though the land itself had decided to listen to the warnings
we'd been ignoring, and, having listened, sent out long green vines
across the dimpled rocks.

Like a lightbulb, I hover over each of your shadows,
and what you did for me, I'll never finish
listing, even after the palm fronds have been hauled away
with the trash, even if I had ten lifetimes to tell it. Paint may
peel, tables may rust, bacon may trap you on your couch.
My favorite problem lies exhausted on the bank of a stream,
best seen just after rain, when the mist is a yellow leaf, quivering
on a branch. If it becomes a trap, let me know.

The Happy Man

1.

I feel like a Disney attraction, freshly
out of sand castles and earrings but
stapled to the convulsive since 1955.

Who are these dwarves,
whose sunset have
they hijacked? It's
time to respect baby buds.

Far from land, a ship sleeps at anchor;
the woman in cabin 255 mutters
in her bunk like a lover betrayed.
In her dream, she takes a bite of fish.

Whoever recalls what took place today
must ignore the sounds my hands
made when I entered her cabin.

2.

The dog I'd been disguised as lay asleep.
Speak, happy man.
I was you in my red velvet dog
mask, whistling Schubert. Ripples fell, a
door popped open and your bag
of secrets spilled onto fresh soil
where carrots and celery grow.

A log leapt off its root system, silver-bright,
alert with blossoms.
That new feeling
fell lightly around you, like a girlfriend.
Petulant feathers filled a meadow as they fell.
The west wind rose with a set of knives
and the purple ceramic bowl of life flowed over.

3.

All day I've been happy, without reason.
Oh, I have cause for melancholy, but
before I surrender to your whim,

I'll have my fun
impersonating a Stoic who would rather
shake villainy onto your pasta than
splash funk onto your migraine's hollow wallet.

The moment you were wedded to earth,
bells pinned you at the foot of a stairs.
Your wastebasket overflowed with pleas, and
your money scattered into
nasturtiums I carry on my back.

I intend no disrespect.
I wish you dreams of angels, larks and bees.

4.

The sun hangs low in the teased sky
and singers insist their love rings true.
When this soft clash between weak birds
(mine red-white and quiet, yours blue-black
and loud) comes to its fated draw, the night, full of
sepia fruit, will shed her clumsy cloak
and let us embrace.
                                        Until that moment
how shall I protect my coins, and what shall
I tell the harpist? Our ancestors cleared
trees, sighing when dusk settled like a
dependable god on the clearing and stacks
of virgin lumber that gave proverbs weight but
wound up coded into mud along with the words.
Hey, they said each voice heard one healing particle.

5.

I look toward the rust-colored ground and find
some friendly stranger's barely legible name
and the readable name of the illusion
that rides it through this land. It binds us
to itself with light green thread
and as mountains melt, storms
emerge over hills like stars. *You*
who have never strayed from
shore, take courage in my
song's allure. The night
has motioned toward the door,
the wind has eaten most leaves from our trees.
Come, friendly strangers,
let us topple into its sticky knowledge.

Only in Theory

Our economy pivoted yesterday morning, and all bunnies began living in newly retrofitted warrens, with tinfoil "I Got Soul" flags visible from the street. Our warren was filled with cases of bar soap and trashcan liners, detergents, all sorts of objects that conjured images of cleanliness and orderly, well-policed boundaries between people. We had no goal except avoiding pain,

but look at how much we caused. We were "history" in the sense of manifesting the clutches of invisible hands. So what if the cosmos united to punish us for crimes we never committed? Fate, evidently, cared neither for our innocence nor our pants. We stood, one behind the other, in the shadow of a telephone pole, the better to glimpse the eclipse before visiting our mother's warren, where a samba band waited for duct tape.

Cardinals and dahlias were starting to open; a dolphin nearly died. I bent over laughing as forty years assumed the shape of a paper airplane. We were punks! Libraries remembered us! We cracked open pineapples as though they were eggs, and made a point of not missing trains.

Before we nodded off, I thanked you for enduring the humiliation of becoming the idiosyncratic person you were destined to be. "Maintaining uniqueness in a conformist age like ours requires more inner chutzpa than most people have, and, my man, I think you have it," I said. I felt taller when I stood next to you, thinner when I sat with you, better when I followed you up hills.

Then the realty bubble popped. I threw myself onto an angel and watched the dead pony parade light up a furious pasture.

In Our Generation

Our world constructed its child
out of broken stars and fresh peaches.
When we were in Mrs. Fee's first-grade class, we
had all the sand we needed. History held clothes in
her left hand, a pencil in her right. I placed my left hand
into the bag of months and picked one. But my eyes
fell onto a dark square of carpet near the door, and stayed there,
hard as they knew how.

We wore wooden lion masks, crayoned abstract
menorahs. Nothing about winter could be misused,
we believed, as ashen haze silvered
the evening. You pulled a book
from your bag: Nabokov, *Speak, Memory.*
I wished the rain could be President.
We were twenty, twenty-one, and our
books pulled at our veins. I rode a bus into town
to deliver my hand-written tragedies, and no one laughed.
The Illustrated Man hung low in the pre-dawn sky.

Among the swaying trees, ribbon-shaped plants grew
bubble-shaped leaves, and men lay heavy burdens there.
I smelled smoke twist through broken chrysanthemums,
wiped pink dust from my eyes. With no
reason to dance, I kept dancing (the Pony, the Swim)
on spiral paths the world offered. I felt warm,
almost awesome.

The wet pavement in front of our dwelling was a broken web.
The world's brain became a dairy farm, where
you lay in an oak-root cradle, clutched by your
ignorance, cowed by the size of our nation's errors.

A Pillowcase Moon

Look at how darkness fell tonight
on the bed where I lay dreaming of you in my
fever. Yet an animal must
die before the ceremony finds
its only possible ending. Fathers try
explaining it to their sons, there in the sacred grove;
their sons stand as though carved out of wood,
sharp fingers budding for the first time. Then
fathers leave or die, the sons get frantic,
they calm down enough to meet and talk.
In a room full of magazines, the 1964 through 1980
crowd gathers; Jesus, they look sad.
What crime did they commit, that they should spend
their gorgeous years in such cubicles, waiting only
to slip into some great body of water and swim
to a distant island of exhausted sleep?

A Quiz About the Moon

I cursed my unmade bed and walked down to the hidden
gardens with a strange new pen in my hand.
The nightingale asked no questions
about clouds obscuring the moon.
Back on the mattress, a faint beam turned to me
and asked about the construction of a heart.
The room's yellow background cheered our sleep, yet
dreams still came floating above the hi-def carnival
like kings in canoes.

The nation became a replica.
I held onto its smooth, public side
and for the first time in a year, heard a box
laugh long and hard – I mean an ordinary cardboard
box, nothing odd-looking, *laugh* at the path I had chosen
through the gorgeous, droning landscape.
Elk, squirrel, hawk: "Watch me," each one said,
and my new pen vanished; my notebook
was only a handful of crumbling eucalyptus leaves.

Yes, I'm the problem, and the problem had issue.
Last year, I saw little holes all around me
like dark stars against a white sky, and I like knowing that you
put them there in some funny way all your own.
The rest of that year was a smooth plank of oak.
This year's a plastic ID badge
pinned where your mouth was.
All our teachers and pastors are humming inside
a permanent green. At just past eleven, with the sun close
to its height, we looked at one another in a way that
assumed we guarded our gems with thorns. But
no human being can purify this world.
Like an eager mouse, I don't
mind my corner, although at times the younger me
pokes my chest in wonderment – it's his corner then.
He has every right to be abrupt.

I suppose a glass of whole milk may arrive, a slice or two
of whole wheat bread, perfect for nervous stomachs,
but the meat I crave involves another past
that leaks, spews and bellows.
And so I write to you, old friend, not with news
about music and the war, but on the back of a duct-tape mural
of faces on a plane the moment they heave up into the sky,
yanked above snowy trees into improvisations
filling ten thousand rooms with soft old light.

If I haven't dreamed it, I cannot want it. If I have dreamed
it, I must bear its weight in my hands
through the packs of dogs and bushels of leaves animating this
landscape. That's why dreams matter: under a sharp moon,
the greedy are slightly punished and sink into the silent ground.
A cactus represents a war within the dreamer, seen through
the lens of regret. No wonder I like my job. Take a look
at it and tell me what you can't attain.

The Secret Contract

What is finally worthy of our praise other than what has given us the opportunity to love? The night wind brings, right here, a slightly more pronounced rhythm in its conversation with surrounding branches. The birds and squirrels that live and feast there view our histories skeptically. The sands of time flow not from hand to hand, nor does the wise man's word pass easily among fools. Sleepers, awake! Turn away no more! A sword glows in the eastern sky.

So what if our heroes all turned out to be scared, damaged, lonely drinkers with bad breath and insomnia? We saw them get up on their horses, trot into town with the provision list, come back with the salt pork and the brogans. I had your address and a nice new pipe, and when the signal arrived, I decoded the blink-pattern right away (it was cake) and radioed in. Next thing I knew, I was airborne and prepped to move from roof to roof through the enemy city at night. I got a new alias every five days.

The last time I visited that city, it seemed even more mysterious than it had when I was an agent and crept awed through its dark patios and mazy corridors looking for the armory, where a sleepy Cuban sergeant would let me "use the bathroom." The walls had been brick or stone. What were they now, some sort of gelatin-silicone something? As suddenly as in a fairy tale, a coyote sprang out from behind a wastebasket and hightailed it out of there, resting finally in the mountain underbrush a few miles outside of town. Meanwhile,

a voice I remembered from a long time before asked me to speak. But a large crowd was dancing to loud eighties rock and no one could have heard me. Yet the others on stage with me, most of them, were staring at me and smiling, waiting for me to rise and greet everyone with inspirational words. Sirens went by; bells rang; tinny cell phones buzzed and chirped. I had this theory about the importance of steering calmly through the swelling waves of something powerfully attractive yet not quite comprehensible, even in outline or premise. The mood became the only artifact. Anyway, you could bemoan it.

One Evening, Years Ago

The little lakes that condensed in my bathroom
became my son's new toys.

Even his special cereal bowl
sometimes refused his spoon.

In front of the boy stood
an explanation in the form of a Moebius strip.

I sit behind him under a florid sun that declared
You have wanted this wet heat since you were a baby.

White curls spilled down my neck in ringlets, like money,
and we both felt grateful for bicycles, cement, rain.

The Fair-Skinned Invaders

The night twists and sprains your sleep,
your surroundings thicken and condense.
Fire, the Springsteen of elements, rubs its knuckles on
your sleepy head: It's whistle-blower day, and you know it.
You watch your nation's history whinny like a horse.

A drunken songbird bites again, hinders a woman
from walking her child down a gentle green slope.
Chickens who would normally be sacrificed
peck at the hem of her ankle-length dress.
Woolen grass frosts the unrefined, soft earth.

One of the rivers that flows into your head
chuckles at your gilded velvet barricade,
then reappears in every part of every house.
It's as if the air had
started growling, its clumsy
bubble suddenly overturned.

You look up at the salted fabric of sky.
From frayed oak branches comes
a ritual squawking.
A clumsy elephant comes lumbering from the coco-plums,
thrashing terraces of roses.
Deer run to places where frogs hide.

Stupid, restless monkeys pick apart exotic plants.
Porcupine drunk, a tight-rope walker
wanders through a desert toward his log house,
finding refuge with other tenant farmers.
A soft ticking's still going inside official calendars.
You study the monkeys, pull seeds out of wreckage.

The tragic muse arrives late, but bears gifts.
Your hero adjusts his hat, clutching
the reins of his stallion. Then
he makes a raft from logs Calypso gave him:
its sail is a valentine that makes him a target.
Your tear a strip of fabric from my shirt and hand it
to him. "Is this an aphrodisiac?" he asks.

Morning's a different fabric strip.
Smooth, shiny men carry rope from women's bedrooms
as remorse hangs over them like
humidity, humility, or something equally terrible.

Thunder arrives in the shape of the king of diamonds.
Pimply men exchange small portable cannons
and pieces of wood for beer. The brewmaster drinks
from the fountain. He knew your
grandfather, whose ring slips lightly off your knuckle.

Aloof in their gem-studded towers, officials tarnish
like antique brass, and the women
of this village lift their toddlers from bramble bushes.
Somewhere between two big rocks, clearly marked, lies
a path only you can miss. And then the law
calls you back to questions you left tangled.

You wind up skeptical in a Bible shop.
Every night you have the dream:
Just as the pretty girl pulls off her dress
a cherub runs her through with a spear.

Heath Ledger, Actor, Dead at 28

I still see room for a sense of the inevitable,
if only as a warning against embroidering the concept
with purple thread and strands of gold, framing a cameo
beyond which no one ventures without
paying the ancient ferryman. In that room I see
another room
and in that room I see a model train burning real coal
and taking actual miniature people away from a depot.
Now, am I confusing imagination with memory here,
or have I stumbled onto a valuable image for how
comfortable we're starting to feel with doom,
how easily
those jonquil plants... Those movie award shows... The
American Youth Soccer Association playoffs... Blessed be their names,
blessed be the names of seasons and their flowers, blessed be trails they
leave hanging above our heads,
blessed be these dented angels pouting in silence above
our neighborhood power grid... Blessed be the hummingbird
sized Buddha
who warned us away from spiders and felonies.
We held our eyes open, afraid to miss one flicker
of imbalance. Now the moon idles, full and glacial,
before taking off, impatient to mourn the other side
of the earth, scaly like ours, and young no longer.

We Made a Deal

I couldn't touch clouds but I knew giants
from dwarves. The assumption was, father
spoke through sons as ink speaks through garments.
At the bottom of this defensiveness, a nine-year-old girl
has clenched my leg and won't let go.
May I pay homage to her fingers, her barrettes, her
white ankle-socks? My last-minute heart,
thrown into disorder by her dazzling music, went young
and stupid on me, and when you're near,
the air I hear swallows my home, and my fingers
grow sleepy and self-radicalized.
The compass needle swings, it is a jazz drummer
gliding through the dark arms of the forbidden,
and the fish tank I carry in my pocket has never
felt missing or paranoid. The tank's blue, the fish gold.
A full moon waits between fish like a cloud shifting in her sleep.
You will like its story, I know. You will use it like a milk bottle
with a body of fire and the knees of a child,
the nearest, strangest, not-yet-named one.
Then I slap myself awake: *Stop talking*
to trees, I say to myself, *your room's unbearable,*
your window's opaque with ice. The hallway light
flickers. It must be an animal from the ocean floor,
lost and hurt. When it comes our turn to die,
only our worst memories will follow us into the afterworld,
cut-up and dirty-tasting, where they turn into the shell
of the eggs we become there, and we move our feet
very slowly over the sidewalk
which is lit with weird evangelical zeal.

One Step Away from Dreams

How would death look if I were a fish?
A pelican soaring from heaven, lifting
me out in a flash of wet white,
a fact lit up from behind?
I would welcome bird-cry voices, bouncing
off my stolen, onion-skin life. They
don't frighten me. I stand straighter
and swim better in their light, never thinking of being
anywhere other than where I am.
I long to try something
the animal who forces me to behave will
not allow. My notions stumble over
antelope and tiger carcasses.
No bull horns blow, no
eclipse clouds the moving sun.
At school, I'm a flying crane,
thinking brightly-colored thoughts:
"Life here's a horse barn in darkness.
Hours and days are soft cotton rags I
hold to my nose with both hands
like melting snow." Birds accomplish
homes in the fading sky. Pale
cream sunshine blends with
evening, ignoring its empty
bed. The northwest sky dances.
The acting becomes real, for a moment.

Down Here on the Ground

The dead possums fill me with the urge to look away from them, toward you. But then, I'm stuck in the bright yellow smiley-face of your despair, from which I find it much harder to look away.

For example, when we spoke on the phone earlier this week, I thought you said you had no money, no books, no shirt. I must have misheard you: here you are, carrying a twenty in your mouth, holding a novel under your arm, and wearing a plain white T-shirt with a hand-shaped aquamarine stain over your heart, which I thought you said was beating arhythmically.

I know you've been renting rooms in Santa Cruz Victorians since 1975, that you own three pairs of blue Levis, seven plain white T-shirts, and two pairs of Keds, that you drink only chocolate milk – no coffee, no tea, no alcohol – and that you work as a part-time janitor in a furniture store, a local newspaper office, and other, sketchier places. But you've become such a mumbler I could only catch about one word in every twelve, and most of them were about jeans, T-shirts, Keds and chocolate milk. Oh, yes – you're rereading Lawrence Durrell's *The Alexandria Quartet*, which you called "my favorite work of detective fiction. I like best the encyclopedic reach of its language and its analysis of love and loss." It took me over an hour to get that sentence out of you, and I had to ask you to repeat several times, even to shout – but your low murmuring mumble continued, with little variation, for a long time.

When you asked for money, I felt heat rising in my belly, and thought I was turning into some sort of tree. I phoned you an hour later, but couldn't make out your mumbling over the flock of loud pink-blue hummingbirds that kept bumping against my window. Each one was a little flaming oval through which I could see the world reunited.

It had become a day for awe and imaginary numbers, for a pit stop on Mulholland Drive, where you can look north or south and see a salad bigger than the math that got you there. I didn't mean "you" as in you, but on a day like this, anyone can intuit the invisible giants who live just above us, the ones who gave us our sexes and professions, who pay some of us so much and others so little. Our years belong not to us, but to them, whether we see them as made of fire or wind. Their legs and arms are the color of the sky. They conceal their genitals so that we may preserve our attention for the more mundane tasks that greet us with smiles and reproaches.

And now the fog they make takes over everything we like, much the way tattoo parlors and check-cashing services take over the smaller, forgotten blocks found in every old downtown. I thought you said you cleaned one of those tattoo places, but you were mumbling again – did you mean you got a tattoo? May I see it? May I unsee it after I see it? I thought you said yes to both things, but the time element doesn't scan. We weren't clarifying. There was no I, only my fugue.

I called you again, long distance on my tinny-sounding flip phone, and asked you for a prayer or ritual chant to be said at the moment of choosing a pair of socks. After all, you are what I would have been had I been born a girl. You said, as best as I could figure after a lot of repetition and please-speak-ups, "Feet, greet your seat and meet the street!" I wrote that down. Out my window, hummingbirds had gone silent, and wore their silence like badges. The dirt looked yellow, used-up. A stand of Joshua trees twisted into a series of numbers (a two, a zero, a five, a three). I had been living in a desert for years – why did I not grasp this terrible fact until now?

In my hand was a stone made of bacon I didn't know whether to throw or eat. Like many men, I knew not where my best interests lay, and only you were qualified to find them, explain them to me, and show me how to live. But where were you? I had been on the phone with you a moment before! And I reached between my legs to find that I had become completely smooth down there, smooth as the back of my own knee.

The Exact Spot

So many of us confused politeness with endorsement
as we gestured with unbought, unsmoked cigars
and felt natural as gravity about every phrase
that came out of us. Night,
an old friend who thinks in particulars,
won our silence
with a plump face – it could have been a man or a woman,
yet we all recognized the mouth-chin combo from
when we walked into town to buy mint.
Priests appeared and began to caw the names
of their favorite foods: Tomatoes, pepperoncini.
In my heart, I joined them for a ride to their cathedral,
wishing to touch some perfect arc there, but so many of us
had been stripped naked, mocked, hosed, or shot
we became squirrels, raccoons, possum, badgers
until we became
our ideal older brothers and sisters,
who came to our town playing and singing on nights
we remembered for years. There could be no other way
but that tall pines would guard our path into
the forest, the one we would take when old enough.

Now, a little sister waits with me in a lobby
of a Brooklyn apartment building, feeling rejected,
like me, and contemplating the curving trees.
Her brother's waiting in a hospital, at the back of
her mind, but he's also here next to me, most all the time.
Kind of Blue plays on repeat with a weird, troubling echo
until it sounds like grief.
                                        All this is happening
before you were born – it's a story written in fountain pen,
lit with candles and moonlight, and birds wake the author

every dawn. Their song enters Brooklyn, too. I look
down again, and the boys are listening to it, in their circles.
I've been erased by the sun, but I put up no struggle.
Besides, I'd never heard birds like that before,
so ancient, so maternal, so adept.

The Knife States its Case

The future is a herd of color-coded porcupines whose migrations present a sequence of detailed instructions for creating personal religious holidays.

The future offers us the parable of the ship with two captains; they argue like angry drunks for the whole voyage, yet the ship docks safely, its hold full of fish.

The future has two ends to its tunnel and no hands are strong enough to guide me from one end through to the other end and out.

The future goes straight down into the place where everything I know becomes useless and rows of mannequins represent all the people I have ever loved.

The future knows us without loving us. In its dark bedroom, I have no signature, no Doors albums, no pills. The future wants to tell me that a woman may be sleeping, and I must not, under any circumstances, wake her up.

In the future, the darkening sky wakes up and pours rain on my photographs while another strange face creeps across most of what I remember.

Solace

Our goateed landlord veiled his oldest tenant's
scarred face with a feather boa.
Weightlifters inched past, burping. Floral
dribbles crawled behind them,
trailing matching berries.

There were stretcher-bearers too, and errors
everyone enjoyed. We both rode empty
planters down the hill, and the whole tradition recognized
my moustache. Pelted by hailstones of mercy, our
reproductive organs bristled and steamed.
We met genuine wizards who studied magic books,
witches who knew the heavy snack of melancholy.

If you see the whole thing as a diagram of how
people learn fear, you grasp the dark persistence
inside the children walking together, holding hands.
The fresh air colors their Tuesday, chills
their walk. We see them in the wind, in a lazy
afternoon, we see them return as the sky falls,
the moon's mirror reflecting the icy and the mute.
Right away, we recognized our first sound
and knew our second would crack open the first.
Screeching followed. The only things we called our own
were smothered in memory, but never learned
to mourn. You knew but forgot your way through
the daydream into the field of favorite tunes, and
were you to awake in the middle of the diagram,
smelly in your overbaked darkness, you'd write the first
thing you see down here, on this old page,
and write it with the light turned on.
When the sky falls next time, and the stars
drop from their convertible orbits, what names will
have gathered in the bottom of a once-empty
dresser drawer! Look at the number of them!

But other children don't want to hear what I memorized. They
leave footprints like torches in the short grass.

Let's follow them into town, into the scary part of our story
where puzzle pieces grab each other and blow whistles.
The pieces and whistles are huge and dangerous, like the men
who own them. The winter wind carries a new, rude story.
Trees lean in it, loving again their sober patchwork,
their skittishness. The meadow tosses me a trowel,
and a great peace suddenly settles in
our bedroom, and in our blood, a path as bright as
the orange sun is marked out by masks on sticks.

Let's inspect the situation: a friendly gaze reveals
crisp silhouettes, healthier than wit, sweeter than
the names of rebels. The year has a function
and I guess my part of it is the same
as yours, the same oak tree tire swing
still in its old position, in front of the same sturdy home.

A few days from now, rain rolls out like the third Fury
but tonight's full Christmas moon
hangs like an apple, lighting a salty haze
that persists like the will to conquer land and build empires.
It's been thirty-three years and the lady
just kept talking about her problems
until the deepest water... The record player... Merging onto
the one-oh-one south... The light that
fades. The grind you love. A circle of leaping doctors.
Information systems layered on top of each other,
having sex and falling asleep.

I am not alone in thinking this. But remember,
I have been an inmate, sleeping beneath a tree
in the middle of a flood. This morning, I am almost
without destination. The buildings look

puffy and convicted.
I stand knee deep in wondering
whether today is Monday or Tuesday, whether
to fish or cut bait. It's easy
to learn from a landscape,
easier if Tuesday's equations fit
the rhythmic pattern of the dream: a noiseless
tiger bears a wood-nymph on her back like an empty chair
across this pleated horizon. I'm an acorn
who wants to think – my tiny brow furrows in a hard,
obsessive shove. The pages of my book, curling
in the moist wind, still look groggy with fear.
She sleepwalks toward a door at the end of a room
but that was part of some other dream, no?
The anxiety I can't shake concerns deeper
connections between room and horizon.
The perfect breeze provided all the distraction
we needed. Further out at sea,
you had noticed ash raining down, and called it feathers
because you saw only the painted side. You
shouted "The world's between my fingers" into
your cupped hands. Dark blue waves replaced the curled
pages in my book of days.

Now the wood-nymph
sits at her desk – I see her through her window.
She counts her cash before putting it in her purse.
All the world is mortal, as it sails, but it feels like whatever
could burn has burned.
The man who drinks from her old cup
has a twin sister who eats from her new bowl.
Just now out of the shower, she
cues up the long cut from side two because
she and her twin brother once splashed their mother
in some mystery jungle that was also a neighbor's pool,
perfect for a minute.

I thank her for inviting me – my tired eyes needed
careless Sunday melancholy full of story and rain.
How skillfully her blues weaves tradition
into breaths the color of blood.

I have given her as much as I can. I have little left,
and my most valuable treasure stands in a mist of
unjudging love. We check each other for tar.
I feel a light wind, but nothing more. How did
this gunk get here? I could close my eyes, nap, dream a mythology
and wake up with a slew of restless remarks I yell into my arm.
Since the revolution fell in a field of lavender, each night has become
a tongue, lingering in a cold, calm wind.

I reconsider my career, the parts of language on my
love-desk forming caves and tunnels, and feel
winglessly faithful to the earth. My anger dies down.
I sit with my father, where it is already autumn, and
all animals have been set free. *Father*, I say,
you have been dead these fifteen years.
No horse in this pasture knows my name,
no tree in the forest has heard my voice.
My dates appear on no calendar, and the music
I hear plays only in my head, for me alone.
I recall my past only in bursts of color
and shouts of angry, frightened men who
were trying to warn me, or harm me,
or both. When I look out on the present,
its comforting surfaces, pulleys
and weights in motion, I feel benign,
my hands open out, and the very
landscape seems to be playing a game
that lasts into the peach-colored twilight.

The future implores me to join him,
offers me a stick of peppermint gum
and points at birds settled into their
nests for the night. "Sunset's long gone,"
he mutters, and I know at that moment
I must love what will kill me, and may
not tunnel beneath it. I think
of Evelyn, the girl in the *Dubliners* story,
her left hand opening and closing in her rocker as street
lights flicker. She's been waiting all day,
feels weak. Branches block her street view.
She removes her shoes. Yet somehow our memory of this
scene turns sour in the telling, for we know the way
her story ends, and cannot keep ourselves from
reading the ending into earlier sections, darkening
their shadows and their roads. What changed
was the morning's mood, stern but tender,
always making sure we didn't forget
the dream. The afternoon arrived like an Uber car
driven by an off-duty celebrity. I pulled myself
closer to the open car door. The off-duty celeb
said "ask me no questions!" I closed my eyes
and let the moon tip-toe around me in the dark,
lingering like a pilgrim before going to meet the
end of his bundle. But the barrel of fish had
the last laugh, and it was too late by then for
the modern human anyway. I breakfasted
on remnants. The kitchen had hardened
as I slept – the table offered no apology
for breaking all those cups. "Return After Wanderings,"
read the headline. We decided to keep the rest
of the story as simple as we could.

Ever since I wrapped my legs around our eye contact
my long grass hands have been laid away
and the women on my mind have sparked unadorned
ripples pooling in the center of my temple – my body
feels split into thirds. I see myself riding
a horse through a wood, sweetness breaking
from the ride itself, a *thank-you-for-coming* inside it
like a kiss. Never let it be said that I'm merely human,
clinging to my curious sunken bowls.
My shoes have rubber soles. I hear water
trickling in the next room as I tie the laces.
This ship's all that matters now, that and my knot:
I've got to make it tight, make sure it can slide.

Permission ripens on a shelf with a banana.
If this be the future, I'm that banana.
I had ridden through mist and wind,
stubble fields where leg-weapons
left sad flowers on the landscape.
Tears fell from a girl who glided past
on what looked like a coffee-soaked plaster
heart-shaped cloud. Cartwheeling satyrs with
five-foot phalloi decorated with crescent moons
and white stars took the rustic stage, and a philosopher
stood among them asking "Where were you raised?"

I walked through hall after hall, stopping at door after door,
looking for the smell of adults.
I examined baked surfaces of sneakers in doorways, coughing
flaps of kites across the thin, blotted sky,
the breeze that came in hot nights to lull us asleep.
I was eighteen years old, and could prove it.
I believed my path was a powerful cake, free of any
markings; when I saw spider webs, I flinched.

An older man's face glided past me in a window. I made
a wish on him, told him, and blushed. I interpreted
my blushing as a beckoning, like a stranger
pushed away from you by traffic, and you know it really could
be love but the moment got rained out, lost as a stone
skimming the water before sinking, and you know traffic
is where attention goes to die, hence the urgent beckoning,
the redness in the blush, deepening all this time. Meanwhile,
deep green trees vanished with the sun, and I saw in those halls
that all in love is fair, and that I was willing to wake and retire early
if he granted my little-boy wish.

Summer glimpsed autumn, and older men clapped
each other's shoulders, each clap firming
their business of skin and hunger. Younger men
emerged from their shared recurring dream of
eggs and a scolding mother who kept repeating
"I am lonely" at the stars. I kept running through
the building, looking for eggs, trying to calm the lonely
mother – I, too, was part of their dream – but every path I took was fake.

The winter, in one sense, barely happened.
To hear the rain run on like a popcorn machine
is to hear the voice of our own death, which got closer each day.
The world blinked three times,
begged to stop turning.
I was productive, avoided flu and puddly ground,
picked only what had fallen.

Still, I can't shake my twentieth century
feeling that the bad guys got
away with some awful crime.
You know how it is: as youngsters,
we were fed infamous, heavy meats
and became adults we would not pardon.

Thinness was the hell our suffering
spooned onto our plates every dinner, our masters' names the black
tongues of their beloved anger. I studied their thick egos,
their whip-knotted, bliss-filled pulses.
I would recognize any of them, were he to step out of the meat-smoke
barbeque haze.
                                        Separation time has arrived now
to find us smothered in little blurred demons
not ours to keep. In the space where we listen
to laments, we breathe sad songs of the trees, our hands,
and what we have done to the trees with them.
The world's omens dislike our love, although our skin tastes of roses
and a moist midnight. But I cannot remember right
now where I'm supposed to be, how to find the child,
how to drive the car to the child, where's the car, the keys,
the shoes and pants. The evening peels itself away from its gift
and stacks itself neatly against a white wall. "How about that?"
you ask me, and I answer nothing as water seeps
into the ancient wooden floor of the dream.
I was the pygmy in the gypsy pavilion
when an organist calmed the water with a look and a chord.
The twilit twigs were full of private meanings for us.
We recognize no interruptions now – twigs are one part of
the great word-circus – yet how often the voice of the past
sings "If You Could See Me Now" in a light contralto.

The dark city I live in belongs to men my age.

The day that has just started to depart, what did it
solve? We know more about what might arrive on the boat
we call The Sky, where the light shifts from pink into
dusty blue. But our pavement's on the verge of turning
into lava, with wet clothing still piled on doorsteps,
and the growing cloud. I'm the dark hump that laughs while you squirt at it
and you are the salty skin of a disappointed instinct,

glazed on the front, temporarily incarcerated in
a cage made of stems, hidden at the edge of a mossy river.
The placid mountain range suggests painless
retirement, but insists you reexamine every childhood
blanket, interview every loving fool. I see no one there
but our disbelieving father, now comfortable, now miserable,
his feelers dark and wiry in morning shadow.

About the author:

JAMES CUSHING, born 1953 in Palo Alto CA, holds a doctorate in English from UC Irvine. In the early 1980s, he hosted a live poetry radio program on KPFK-FM in Los Angeles which gave early exposure to Dennis Cooper, David Trinidad, Amy Gerstler, Wanda Coleman, Leland Hickman, and many others. Since 1989, he has taught literature and creative writing at Cal Poly, San Luis Obispo, and served as the community's Poet Laureate for 2008 – 2010. His poems have appeared in many journals, and Cahuenga Press has published four collections: *You and the Night and the Music* (1991), *The Length of an Afternoon* (1999), *Undercurrent Blues* (2004) and *Pinocchio's Revolution* (2010). Cushing currently hosts weekly jazz and rock programs on the college's radio station, KCPR-FM (www.kcpr.org). His daughter is the New York-based poet Iris Cushing.

Also by Cahuenga Press

Specific Mysteries
by Holly Prado, 1991 (OP)

You and the Night and the Music
by James Cushing, 1991 (OP)

Ordinary Snake Dance
by Phoebe MacAdams, 1994
(no ISBN) $10

The Ragged Vertical
by Harry E. Northup, 1996
(ISBN 978-0-9649240-0-0) $15

Sacrifice
by Cecilia Woloch, 1997
(ISBN 978-0-9649240-4-8) $12

Esperanza: Poems for Orpheus
by Holly Prado, 1998
(ISBN 978-0-9649240-5-5) $12

The Length of an Afternoon
by James Cushing, 1999
(ISBN 978-0-9649240-6-2) $12

Homelands
by Jonathan Cott, 2000
(ISBN 978-0-9649240-7-9) $12

Dreaming the Garden
by Ann Stanford, 2001
(ISBN 978-0-9649240-8-6) $15

Reunions
by Harry E. Northup, 2001
(ISBN 978-0-9649240-9-3) $15

Tsigan
by Cecilia Woloch, 2002
(ISBN 978-0-9715519-0-9) $13

Livelihood
by Phoebe MacAdams, 2003
(ISBN 978-0-9715519-1-6) $12

These Mirrors Prove It
by Holly Prado, 2004
(ISBN 978-0-9715519-3-0) $20

Undercurrent Blues
by James Cushing, 2005
(ISBN 978-0-9715519-4-7) $15

Red Snow Fence
by Harry E. Northup, 2006
(ISBN 978-0-9715519-5-4) $15

Strange Grace
by Phoebe MacAdams, 2007
(ISBN 978-0-9715519-6-1) $15

From One to the Next
by Holly Prado, 2008
(ISBN 978-0-9715519-7-8) $15

Pinocchio's Revolution
by James Cushing, 2009
(ISBN 978-0-9715519-8-5) $15

Where Bodies Again Recline
by Harry E. Northup, 2011
(ISBN 978-0-9715519-9-2) $15

Touching Stone
by Phoebe MacAdams, 2012
(ISBN 978-0-9851843-0-8) $15

Oh, Salt/ Oh, Desiring Hand
by Holly Prado, 2014
(ISBN: 978-0-9851843-1-5) $15

The Magicians' Union
by James Cushing, 2014
(ISBN 978-0-9851843-2-2) $15

East Hollywood:
Memorial to Reason
by Harry E. Northup, 2015
(ISBN: 978-0-9851843-6-0) $20

The Large Economy of the Beautiful:
New and Selected Poems
by Phoebe MacAdams, 2016
(ISBN 978-0-9851843-8-4) $20

For each book ordered,
add $5.50 (shipping & handling)
and send to:
Cahuenga Press
1256 North Mariposa Avenue
Los Angeles, CA 90029

Most titles also available from:
Small Press Distribution
1341 Seventh Ave.
Berkeley, CA 94710